Let Freedom Ring

The Battles of Lexington and Concord

By Judith Peacock

Consultant:
S. Lawrence Whipple
Lexington Town Historian
Lexington Historical Society
Lexington, Massachusetts

Bridgestone Books
an imprint of Capstone Press
Mankato, Minnesota

Bridgestone Books are published by Capstone Press,
151 Good Counsel Drive • P.O. Box 669 • Mankato, Minnesota 56002.
www.capstonepress.com

Printed in the United States of America

Library of Congress Cataloging-in-Publication Data
Peacock, Judith, 1942–
    The battles of Lexington and Concord / by Judith Peacock.
        p. cm. — (Let freedom ring)
    Includes bibliographical references and index.
    ISBN 0-7368-1096-X (hardcover)
    ISBN 0-7368-4491-0 (paperback)
    1. Lexington, Battle of, 1775—Juvenile literature. 2. Concord, Battle of, 1775—Juvenile
literature. [1. Lexington, Battle of, 1775. 2. Concord, Battle of, 1775. 3. United States—
History—Revolution, 1775–1783—Campaigns.] I. Title. II. Series.
E241.L6 P43 2002
973.3′31—dc21   2001005004

Summary: Discusses the events that led the British and the colonists in America to clash in
    the Battles of Lexington and Concord. Describes the actions of both the Patriots and the
    British on April 19, 1775, when the battles that began the American Revolution occurred.

Editorial Credits
Rebecca Aldridge, editor; Kia Bielke, cover designer, interior layout designer, and interior
illustrator; Jennifer Schonborn, cover production designer; Jo Miller, photo researcher

Photo Credits
Cover: Bettmann/CORBIS; Hulton/Archive Photos, 5, 36; North Wind Picture Archives, 9,
14, 18, 29, 39; DVIC and National Archives, 13, 43; Index Stock Imagery/Paul Rocheleau,
11; Stock Montage, 17, 33; Index Stock Imagery/Jonathan Kannair, 21; PhotoSphere
Images/PhotoQuest, 22; Index Stock Imagery/Tim Lynch, 24–25; Robert Holmes/CORBIS,
27; Index Stock Imagery/Steven Alexander, 31; Lee Snider/CORBIS, 35; Kelly/Mooney
Photography/CORBIS, 41

1   2   3   4   5   6   07   06   05   04   03   02

Table of Contents

Chapter One

Road to Revolution

On the evening of April 18, 1775, farmers throughout the colony of Massachusetts went to bed. They thought the next morning would be like any other. They would pick up their plows and work their fields. However, there was to be no plowing on April 19.

After midnight, word spread throughout the countryside that British soldiers were on the march. Farmers, along with shopkeepers, craftsmen, and other citizen soldiers, grabbed their guns and gunpowder. They hurried to protect the villages of Lexington and Concord. The shots fired later that April day signaled the beginning of the American Revolutionary War (1775–1783).

The Trouble Begins

The trouble between the 13 American colonies and Britain began earlier than 1775. In 1763, the French and Indian War (1754–1763) came to an end.

The Battle of Lexington came as a surprise to both colonists and British soldiers. Neither side had been planning on a war.

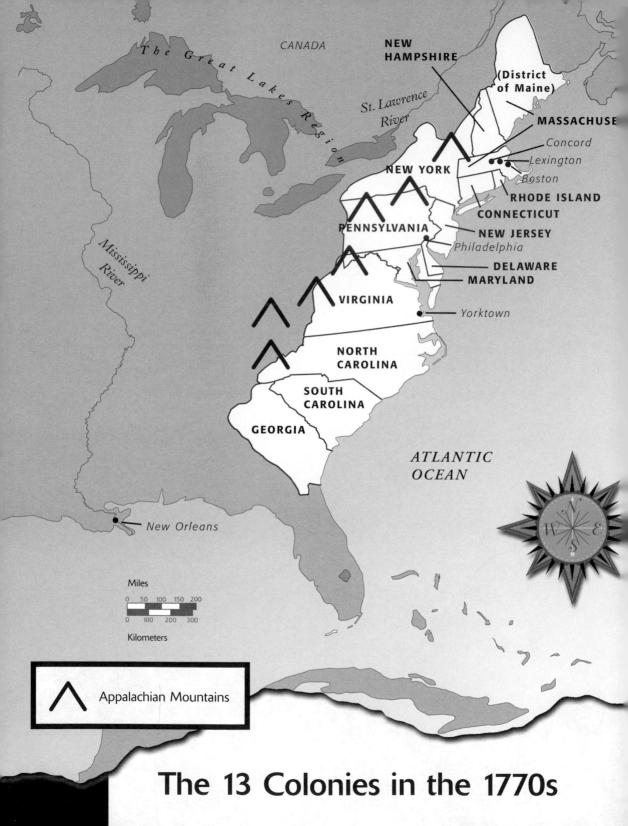

The 13 Colonies in the 1770s

CANADA

The Great Lakes Region

St. Lawrence River

NEW HAMPSHIRE

(District of Maine)

MASSACHUSE

Concord
Lexington
Boston

NEW YORK

RHODE ISLAND
CONNECTICUT

PENNSYLVANIA

NEW JERSEY
Philadelphia

DELAWARE
MARYLAND

Mississippi River

VIRGINIA

Yorktown

NORTH CAROLINA

SOUTH CAROLINA

GEORGIA

ATLANTIC OCEAN

New Orleans

Miles
0 50 100 150 200
0 100 200 300
Kilometers

Appalachian Mountains

Britain and its American colonies had defeated France and its American Indian friends. After the war, King George III wanted the colonies to help pay Britain's huge war debt. He also wanted them to contribute to the costs of keeping troops in America.

The colonists disliked the tax laws used to raise this money. These laws required colonists to pay taxes on goods they bought from Britain. Many colonists boycotted, or refused to buy, British goods. British merchants lost money because of the boycott, so the British government repealed, or took back, many of the laws. The colonists' actions, however, angered King George III, who looked for more ways to control the colonies.

Tensions Mount

The loudest protests took place in Massachusetts, especially in the seaport of Boston. Three of the most active opponents of British policy lived in Boston. These Patriots were Samuel Adams, John Hancock, and Dr. Joseph Warren.

Adams had started secret groups in Boston known as the Sons of Liberty. These groups

Patriots vs. Loyalists

In 1775, only about one-third of all colonists were Patriots in support of independence from Britain. People who were loyal to the British government were called Tories or Loyalists. Some of them were spies for the British.

encouraged noisy demonstrations, mob attacks on tax collectors, and street fights with British troops. The Sons of Liberty had to be careful. If they were caught, the British government might condemn them as traitors and hang them.

Boiling Point

The quarrel between the colonists and their British rulers soon reached the boiling point. On the night of December 16, 1773, about 50 members of the Sons of Liberty, inspired by Adams, disguised themselves as Mohawk Indians. They boarded three British ships in Boston Harbor and dumped 342 chests of tea into the water. They did this to protest the British government's policies on tea.

The king and Parliament reacted harshly to news of the Boston Tea Party. Parliament ordered Boston's harbor to be shut down, which hurt the city's economy. More British troops were sent to keep order. Lieutenant General Thomas Gage, commander of the British troops in the colonies, became military governor of Massachusetts.

The Fuse Is Lit

Events in Boston shocked people in all the colonies. Most colonists hoped for a peaceful settlement of

The true Sons of Liberty

And Supporters of the Non-Importation Agreement,

ARE determined to refent any the leaft Infult or Menace offer'd to any one or more of the feveral Committees appointed by the Body at Faneuil-Hall, and chaftife any one or more of them as they deferve ; and will alfo fupport the Printers in any Thing the Committees fhall defire them to print.

☞AS a Warning to any one that fhall affront as aforefaid, upon fure Information given, one of thefe Advertifements will be pofted up at the Door or Dwelling-Houfe of the Offender.

HANDBILL.

This image shows a handbill written by the Sons of Liberty that supports the boycott of British goods. Sons of Liberty groups eventually sprang up in other colonies besides Massachusetts.

their differences with Britain. But armed conflict with the British seemed likely. For the next 16 months, colonists prepared to defend themselves. Towns regularly drilled their militias. These groups of armed men protected their towns from danger. The colonists gathered guns, ammunition, and food.

British spies told General Gage about the military buildup in Massachusetts. On April 14, 1775, the general received orders from Britain to act against the rebels.

General Gage chose Lieutenant Colonel Francis Smith to lead about 700 soldiers to Concord, 19 miles (31 kilometers) west of Boston. Gage believed Concord was a central location for colonial war supplies. The general's goal was to seize the hidden goods. On the way, the troops would march through several towns, including Lexington.

General Gage did not want to start a war with the American colonists. Instead, he hoped to frighten colonists in Massachusetts and elsewhere with the power of the British army. This show of force, he thought, would discourage them from resisting British rule.

At about 10:00 at night on April 18, 1775, the British soldiers, or Redcoats as the colonists called them, began assembling in Boston's Back Bay. They then filed into boats for a trip across the Charles River. Once on shore, the soldiers would begin their march. Only a few officers, including Gage and Smith, knew Concord was the destination. The mission was supposed to be top secret.

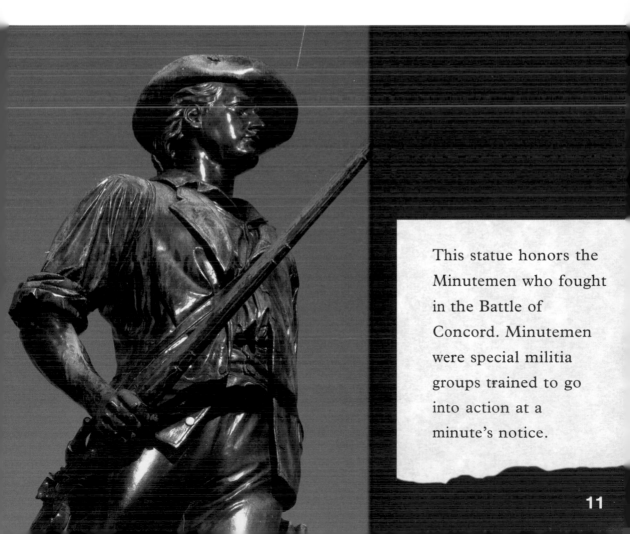

This statue honors the Minutemen who fought in the Battle of Concord. Minutemen were special militia groups trained to go into action at a minute's notice.

Chapter Two

Midnight Riders

Patriot spies in Massachusetts found out the route of the British march. These spies rushed to tell Dr. Joseph Warren. When he heard the news, Dr. Warren sent William "Billy" Dawes and Paul Revere to warn Lexington and Concord.

Dr. Warren gave Dawes and Revere different routes. Dawes's route to Concord was entirely over land. Revere was to go to Lexington by a combined water and land route. Dr. Warren knew that British patrols in the countryside would stop colonial messengers. Sending two messengers by different routes improved chances that at least one would get through.

Paul Revere

Paul Revere was a well-known silversmith in Boston. He made items such as teapots, cups, and plates out of silver. Revere also was a regular messenger for the Sons of Liberty. He often carried news about

Paul Revere was a regular messenger for the Sons of Liberty. On the night of April 18, 1775, he rode through the countryside (above) to warn colonists of British troops on the march.

Boston Patriots to nearby towns and colonies, such as New York and Pennsylvania.

In the days before the march, Revere suspected that the British were up to something. So he made plans with Patriots in Charlestown, across the river from Boston. They were to watch the steeple of a church at the north end of Boston. If the Patriots saw one light, that meant the British

This is the steeple of the Old North Church. Lanterns were placed here to signal the route British troops took on their march.

A Lovely Spy

Margaret Kemble Gage was married to General Gage. She had mixed loyalties for both Britain and the Patriots. It is possible that she was one of many spies who told Dr. Warren about the British plans to march.

were coming by land. If they saw two lights, that meant the troops were coming by water.

As soon as Revere got his orders from Dr. Warren, he sent a message to the caretaker of Old North Church. The caretaker hung two lanterns in the church's steeple. The signal told Patriots in Charlestown the route the British were taking.

When Revere stepped off the boat in Charlestown, a fast horse was waiting for him. Revere jumped on the horse's back and thundered off to warn people of the British foot soldiers' approach. All the way to Lexington, Revere told the captains of militias in various towns, "The regulars are coming out!"

The Regulars

British foot soldiers were called regulars. They marched in a column, usually two by two. The fastest soldiers were used as flankers. These men ran along the side of the road and in front of the regular soldiers. They protected the other British troops from sniper, or hidden, fire.

When Revere reached Lexington, a town 12 miles (19 kilometers) west of Boston and 7 miles (11 kilometers) east of Concord, it was midnight. He immediately went to the home of the Reverend Jonas Clarke, where Samuel Adams and John Hancock were staying. Revere thought the British might be coming to arrest the revolutionary leaders. He warned them to get out of Lexington at once.

William Dawes

William Dawes was a tanner. His job working with leather took him throughout Boston, so he knew how to get around the town well. Dawes also was good at acting. The British stationed guards to check people going in and out of Boston. On the night of his ride, Dawes pretended to be a drunken farmer returning home after a night on the town. His act worked, and the guards let him by.

Like Revere, Dawes raced across the countryside. He shouted and woke up militias in towns and farms all along his route. Dawes arrived in Lexington about 30 minutes after Revere did.

In Lexington, British troops were looking for John Hancock (shown at left). He was a Patriot who was fighting British rule.

Two Riders Become Three

After a brief rest, Revere and Dawes got on their horses again and headed for Concord. Samuel Prescott joined them. Prescott, another Son of Liberty, was a young doctor from Concord.

Not far from Lexington, a British patrol on horseback stopped the three riders. Dawes and Prescott escaped, but Revere was captured and threatened with arrest.

Of the three riders, only Prescott made it to Concord. He arrived at 2:30 in the morning, after

When captured, Revere told a lie to frighten the British troops. He said that 500 Minutemen were between the British troops and Boston. The concerned soldiers hurried toward Lexington, bringing Revere with them.

riding at breakneck speed, shouting all the way. Dawes had been thrown from his scared horse and returned to Lexington on foot. Revere, too, found his way back after the British let him go.

A Secret No Longer

Meanwhile, it was 2:00 in the morning before the British came ashore in Cambridge and the march got under way. There had not been enough boats to take the troops across the river in one trip. When Colonel Smith and his men finally headed toward Lexington, houses all along the road were lighted, even though it was still hours before sunrise. Obviously, the mission was no longer a secret.

"Paul Revere's Ride"

Most Americans believe that Paul Revere was the only messenger on the night of April 18, 1775. This idea comes mainly from a famous poem called "Paul Revere's Ride." Henry Wadsworth Longfellow wrote the poem in 1861. It glorifies Revere but fails to mention William Dawes and Samuel Prescott. The poem contains other mistakes as well. For example, it says that Revere warned the people of Concord. Revere never got that far. However, the poem remains popular because it captures the excitement of that evening.

Chapter Three

Lexington Green

The news that Paul Revere and William Dawes brought created great excitement in Lexington. The clanging bell in the tower on Lexington Green woke many of Lexington's 750 residents, including the local militia. These men quickly gathered on the green. By 1:00 in the morning, about 70 men filled this open, grassy triangle in the middle of town.

Predawn Confusion

Two hours went by with no sign of the British, so Captain John Parker dismissed the militia. Just before dawn, Captain Parker sent out another scout. The rider returned and reported that the British were less than 30 minutes away and marching fast. Parker immediately ordered Lexington's young drummer to beat the call to arms.

After hearing this signal, the militiamen scrambled back to the green. The men kept as far

John Parker was a tall, husky veteran of the French and Indian War. At the time of the Lexington battle, he was ill with a lung disease called tuberculosis. Still, Parker insisted on carrying out his duty to protect Lexington. He died the following September.

Fife and Drum

Music played an important part in military life during the American Revolution. The fife, a flutelike instrument, and drum helped British and American soldiers march in step and lifted their spirits. The drum sounded commands such as the call to arms or the call to cease fire. The drummer usually was a teenage boy. Often, he was the younger brother of a soldier in the troop. William Diamond, about age 18, beat the drum for the Lexington militia. The photo below shows modern-day actors with a drum like the ones played during the American Revolution.

from the road to Concord as possible, hoping that the British would march past.

Around 5:00 in the morning, the first column of Redcoats appeared. The rising sun shone against the long barrels of their musket guns. The king's army was an impressive sight.

The Battle of Lexington

Mounted on horseback, Major John Pitcairn, second in command to Colonel Smith, rode onto the green. Behind him were about 200 foot soldiers. Smith and the main group of soldiers waited on the road. When Major Pitcairn saw that the colonists had guns, he and other officers raced toward the militia. They yelled at the militia to disperse, or break up. "Lay down your arms!" the officers shouted.

The advancing soldiers greatly outnumbered Lexington's small force. Captain Parker ordered his men to turn around and disperse without firing. Their safety was more important than an attempt to stop the British. Patriots left the green slowly but without putting down their guns.

Neither the American colonists nor the British wanted to be the first to fire shots. Yet somehow, from somewhere, a gun went off. To this day, no one knows if the gunshot came from the American side or the British side.

That first shot set off a wild free-for-all. The British soldiers began shooting at the retreating Americans. The Americans fired back. Major Pitcairn tried to stop his men from shooting, but they were out of control. Finally, Colonel Smith ordered a drummer to beat the signal to stop shooting. The British soldiers gradually put their

When the smoke cleared after the Battle of Lexington, seven men from Lexington and one man from a neighboring town lay dead or dying. This modern-day reenactment shows how the battle may have looked in 1775.

Major John Pitcairn

Major John Pitcairn was well liked, even by Boston's Patriots. General Gage purposely chose Pitcairn for the march to Concord. He thought that the Patriots would listen to Pitcairn if the two sides became involved in peace talks. Pitcairn was shot and killed at the Battle of Bunker Hill, only two months after the Battle of Lexington.

guns on their shoulders and got back into position. Eight colonists were dead or dying.

March to Concord

Colonel Smith's officers urged him to return to Boston. Even though Lexington's Patriots had been put down, the officers saw trouble ahead. They said news of the fight at Lexington was certain to bring thousands of Minutemen to the area.

Colonel Smith saw no reason to go back. He intended to follow his orders. With drums beating and fifes playing, the British troops continued their march to Concord.

Chapter Four

Concord's North Bridge

After Prescott alerted them, the people of Concord spent the night hiding gunpowder, guns, and food. In the early morning, 400 Minutemen and militiamen from Concord and neighboring towns assembled in front of Wright's Tavern. Colonel James Barrett, a 65-year-old veteran of the French and Indian War, was in charge.

Outnumbered

About 7:00 in the morning, a scout returned who had seen the fighting in Lexington. His report shocked and angered the people of Concord.

Barrett quickly positioned most of his men along a ridge that overlooked the road to Concord. He sent one company down the road toward Lexington to meet the British. The colonel hoped this show of force would persuade the British to turn back. Instead, Redcoats moved toward the Americans on the ridge and charged

North Bridge was the site of bloodshed in the Battle of Concord. This picture shows a replica, or copy, of the original bridge.

the Americans in the road. Barrett saw that his men were outnumbered and ordered them to retreat.

Growing Numbers

By 8:00 in the morning, British soldiers occupied Concord. Colonel Smith and Major Pitcairn ordered soldiers to search houses and public buildings for war supplies. About 100 men kept guard on North Bridge, which spanned the Concord River. Anyone going to or from Concord had to cross the bridge.

Meanwhile, more Minutemen streamed into the area. Within a short time, the American ranks grew. They gathered on Punkatasset Hill, which overlooked North Bridge. The men watched the Redcoats below and waited for a signal to act.

The Battle of Concord

The British search yielded little. The citizens of Concord had found clever hiding places for their war supplies. For example, some farmers hid weapons and ammunition in newly plowed fields and under piles of animal waste.

The Redcoats did find some wooden gun carriages used to move cannons. The soldiers piled these in the street and started a fire with them. Smoke soon drifted over the rooftops of Concord.

About 9:30 in the morning, the militia on Punkatasset Hill saw the smoke. They thought the British had set the town on fire. The men marched down the hill to save Concord from the British.

Isaac Davis, the 30-year-old captain of the Acton, Massachusetts, Minutemen, led the march. As the Minutemen passed, Barrett warned them not to fire first at the British. Barrett hoped the

Several companies of soldiers were sent to search Colonel Barrett's home (shown here) for war supplies.

Ready, Aim, Fire

American militias were trained to aim their guns directly at individual enemy soldiers. The British were not. Instead, their strategy was to use huge volleys. They fired as much as possible into a group without shooting at specific men.

Redcoats guarding North Bridge would let the militiamen pass by if they did not shoot.

The sight of hundreds of armed men approaching jolted the Redcoats. They retreated to the far side of the bridge and raised their guns. The Patriots were coming fast. Without orders, some British regulars fired at the militiamen.

Captain Davis and one of his young soldiers fell to the ground dead. The Patriots fired at the British, killing two regulars and an officer and wounding four regulars and four officers.

Retreat

Colonel Smith's men did not begin firing at the colonists again. The Concord raid had not been successful, and the British had suffered unexpected losses at the hands of the Patriots.

The longer the British stayed, the more time the Patriots had to build their forces. Colonel Smith organized his troops. They then left, leaving their dead and wounded behind. Their only escape route back to Boston would be the long, narrow road they had traveled earlier.

Minutemen (shown here in a modern re-enactment) rushed to North Bridge and Concord at the sight of a fire in the town.

Chapter Five

Battle Road

The British troops left Concord at noon. The exhausted soldiers marched in a long column of silence. They thought their troubles were over, but they were wrong.

Concord to Lexington

Just outside Concord, Americans started shooting at the British. Militiamen fired at the Redcoats from behind stone walls, trees, boulders, and farm buildings. These American snipers fired off a shot and then raced ahead to find another hiding place from which to shoot. One by one, the Redcoats began falling in the dust.

The American attack confused the British, who had been trained to fight on open ground. British soldiers were not used to an unseen enemy. Flankers ran to the sides of the marching column, trying to flush out the Patriots. However, the flankers were driven back by gunfire.

Battle Road was the route that the British took to Boston on their retreat from Concord. Many British soldiers lost their lives on Battle Road as militiamen hidden in the countryside around them fired shots.

Lord Hugh Percy

At age 32, Lord Hugh Percy was one of the richest men in Britain and a well-respected officer. Like other British officers, Percy considered the American militia to be an unorganized mob. His opinion changed on Battle Road. Percy warned the British government that Americans were skilled fighters and better prepared than anyone thought.

Lexington

The Redcoats arrived in Lexington at 2:00 in the afternoon. Only a few hours earlier, they had left in triumph. Now it appeared they would need to give up or lose their lives.

Suddenly, loud British cheers filled the air. In the distance, a long line of British Redcoats was approaching from the direction of Boston. General Gage had sent 1,000 fresh troops to help Colonel Smith's men. Brigadier General Lord Hugh Percy commanded the relief force. He brought with him two cannons and plenty of ammunition.

Percy quickly took charge and ordered the cannons to be fired. The cannon fire temporarily drove the Patriots back. While the British troops rested and regrouped, the colonial troops organized.

Lexington to Boston

The British troops were back on the road at 3:00 that afternoon. The soldiers still had 12 miles (19 kilometers) to go to reach Boston. Despite the relief troops, the danger for the British continued. General William Heath was now in charge of all the American militias. His plan of attack kept thousands of men firing at the Redcoats.

The British used cannons like this one to drive back the American Patriots.

To keep his men from being slaughtered, Percy ordered flanking troops to break into houses and taverns along the road and search for gunmen. He also ordered them to set buildings on fire so snipers could not hide in them. The soldiers looted and burned hundreds of homes and killed both armed and unarmed occupants.

The British column reached Menotomy, a town halfway between Lexington and Charlestown, at 4:30 in the afternoon. Major fighting occurred here when the Redcoats faced more than 4,000

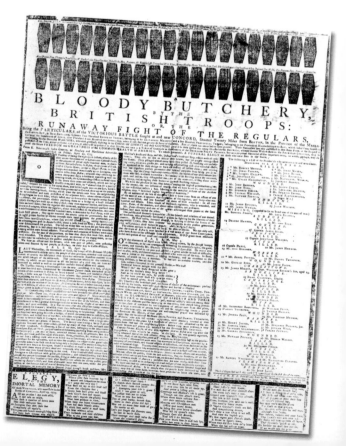

This printed sheet tells the story of the Patriots killed in the Battle of Concord. The sheet was printed many times to spread news of the event throughout the 13 colonies.

Casualties

Despite all the shooting down Battle Road, the number of killed and wounded was low by modern standards. Of the British troops, 73 were killed, 174 were wounded, and 26 were missing. Of the American militiamen, 49 were killed, 39 were wounded, and five were missing.

The low number of casualties was due in part to the weapons used. Guns of that time were not rifled, or grooved, as they are today. Musket balls, or bullets, were poorly shaped. As a result, it was hard to hit anything beyond 50 to 60 yards (46 to 55 meters).

militiamen. When the Battle of Menotomy was over, 40 British regulars and 25 Americans were dead.

At 7:00 in the evening, the British troops finally staggered into Charlestown, where the cannons of the British ship *Somerset* provided them with protection. The colonials stopped firing, and boats took the Redcoats to their camps across the Charles River. Since they last crossed the river, many of the soldiers had marched 35 miles (56 kilometers). All had seen terrible events in the last 20 hours.

Chapter Six

The Revolution Begins

The mounting tensions between Britain and the American colonies exploded in violence at Lexington and Concord. Blood had been shed on both sides. Petitions, boycotts, demonstrations, and other peaceful protests would no longer be enough. A full-scale war seemed certain.

The Colonies Join Together

After the Battles of Lexington and Concord, the Massachusetts militias did not go home. Instead, they camped on the hills around Boston. As news of the events spread during the next two weeks, volunteers from other colonies joined them. Soon about 20,000 militiamen surrounded Boston.

On May 10, 1775, representatives from each of the 13 colonies met in Philadelphia. They voted to form an army to fight against Britain. George Washington became commander of the Continental Army.

The Battle of Lexington and the Battle of Concord (shown here) helped to pull the 13 colonies closer together.

"The Shot Heard Round the World"

*By the rude bridge that
arched the flood,
Their flag to April's breeze
unfurled,
Here once the embattled
farmers stood,
And fired the shot heard
round the world.*

These words from "The
Concord Hymn" by poet
Ralph Waldo Emerson
were first sung at the
dedication of the Concord
Monument on April 19,
1836. The line "And fired
the shot heard round the
world" has become
famous. It means that the
American Revolution has
inspired other countries to
fight for their freedom.

American Revolution

On July 4, 1776, representatives
from the 13 American colonies
signed the Declaration of
Independence. The Declaration
was a formal statement of the
Americans' reasons for breaking
all ties with Britain.

The Revolutionary War
was long and bloody. In 1781,
its last major battle took place
at Yorktown, Virginia. There,
the colonial army defeated
the British.

The Battles of Lexington
and Concord have been called a
turning point in history. On
that April day, Patriots took up
arms to defend their freedom.
They had no idea they were
starting a war for independence
that would result in the birth of
a new nation.

Lexington and Concord Today

The photo below shows people today reenacting the British march that occurred in 1775. Today, Lexington and Concord are suburbs of Boston. In only 30 minutes, people can travel the distance that it took British soldiers several hours to march.

TIMELINE

Americans defeat the British in the Battle of Yorktown.

The Declaration of Independence is signed.

French and Indian War ends.

Boston Tea Party

| 1763 | 1773 | 1775 | 1776 | 1781 |

April 14: General Gage receives orders from the British government to act against Massachusetts Patriots.

April 18

10:00 p.m.	British troops prepare to cross the Charles River.
Midnight	Paul Revere reaches Lexington. William Dawes arrives 30 minutes later.

April 19

1:00 a.m.	The Lexington militia assembles on Lexington Green.
2:00 a.m.	The British march begins.
5:00 a.m.	British soldiers fight with militiamen on Lexington Green.
8:00 a.m.	British soldiers occupy Concord and search for war supplies.
Noon	The British begin retreat to Boston. American militiamen follow them.
2:00 p.m.	The Redcoats reach Lexington. Percy and his troops rescue them.
3:00 p.m.	Percy resumes the march back to Boston. The Americans continue their constant shooting.
7:00 p.m.	The British reach the safety of Charlestown.

Paul Revere's Ride

And yet, through the gloom and the light,
The fate of a nation was riding that night;
And the spark struck out by that steed, in his flight,
Kindled the land into flame with its heat.

Glossary

boycott (BOI-kot)—to refuse to buy certain products or have dealings with certain people as a form of protest

casualty (KAZH-oo-uhl-tee)—someone who is killed, wounded, or lost in action during a war

disperse (diss-PURSS)—to scatter

flanker (FLANG-kur)—a British soldier who ran alongside and in front of other British foot soldiers to provide protection from hidden gunmen

green (GREEN)—a grassy park in the center of a town or village

militia (muh-LISH-uh)—a group of citizens who are trained to fight but serve only in times of emergency

minuteman (MIN-it-man)—a volunteer soldier in the American Revolution who was ready to fight at a minute's notice

musket (MUHSS-kit)—a gun with a long barrel

Parliament (PAR-luh-muhnt)—the lawmaking body of government in Britain

Patriot (PAY-tree-uht)—an American colonist unhappy with British rule

regular (REG-yuh-lur)—a foot soldier in the British army

repeal (ri-PEEL)—to do away with something officially, such as a law

For Further Reading

Branse, J. L. *A Day in the Life of a Colonial Soldier.* The Library of Living and Working in Colonial Times. New York: PowerKids Press, 2002.

Collier, Christopher, and James Lincoln Collier. *The American Revolution, 1763–1783.* Drama of American History. New York: Benchmark Books, 1998.

King, David. *Lexington and Concord.* Battlefields across America. New York: Twenty-First Century Books, 1997.

Todd, Anne. *The Revolutionary War.* America Goes to War. Mankato, Minn · Capstone Books, 2001.

Places of Interest

Buckman Tavern
1 Bedford Street
Lexington, MA 02420
Headquarters for Captain John
Parker and the Lexington militia
while waiting for the British

Bullet Hole House
Monument Street
Concord, Massachusetts
Here a hole can still be seen from
a bullet fired during the battle at
North Bridge.

Captain John Parker Statue
On the green in Lexington,
Massachusetts
Honors Parker and the brave
Americans who fought in the
Battle of Lexington

Concord Museum
200 Lexington Road
Concord, MA 01742
Features items from the American
Revolutionary War

Hancock-Clarke House
Hancock Street
Lexington, Massachusetts
The house to which Paul Revere
rode to warn Adams and
Hancock of the British approach

Minute Man Memorial
At North Bridge in
Concord, Massachusetts
Statue honoring the colonial men
who fought in Concord

**Minute Man
National Historical Park**
Located in Concord, Lincoln,
and Lexington, Massachusetts
http://www.nps.gov/mima
Includes a stretch of Battle Road

Munroe Tavern
1332 Massachusetts Avenue
Lexington, MA 02420-3809
Headquarters of Lord Hugh
Percy on April 19, 1775

North Bridge
Concord, Massachusetts
A copy of the original North
Bridge, the first place Patriots
killed British soldiers

Internet Sites

**Do you want to learn more about
The Battles of Lexington and Concord?**
Visit the FactHound at *www.facthound.com*

FactHound can track down many sites to help you. All the
FactHound sites are hand-selected by our editors. FactHound will
fetch the best, most accurate information to answer your questions.

IT'S EASY! IT'S FUN!
1) Go to *www.facthound.com*
2) Type in: **073681096X**
3) Click on **FETCH IT** and FactHound will put you on the trail
   of several helpful links.

You can also search by subject or book title. So, relax
and let our pal FactHound do the research for you!

Index